The Role of Productivity in Community Success: The Jesuit-Guaraní Cultural Confluence

David Satterlee

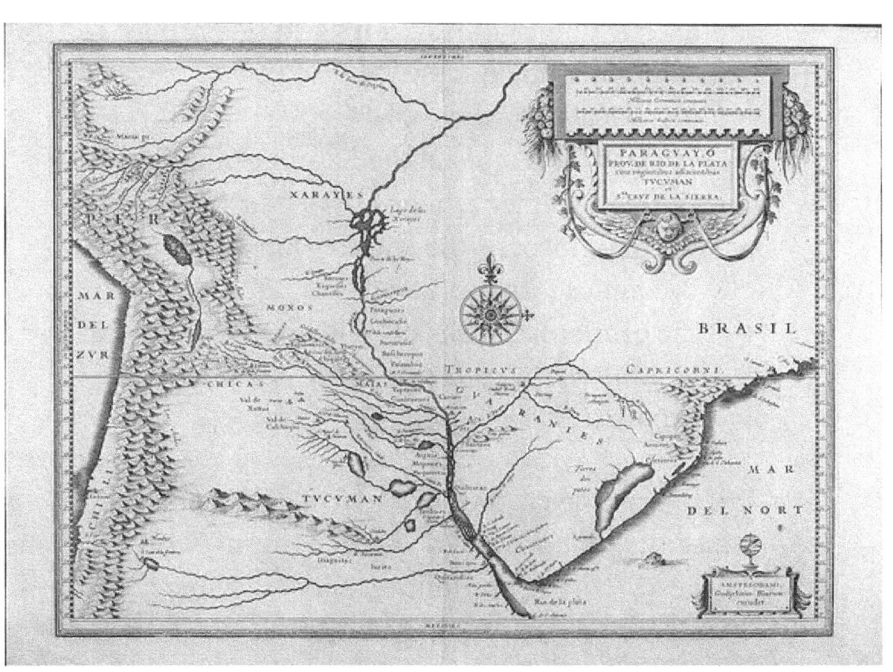

Blaeu, W.J. - *Paraguay, o Prov. de Rio de la Plata cum regionibus adiacentibus Tucuman et S.ta Cruz de la Sierra*, published in Amsterdam, 1645

This is a **living parable for our changing world**, now suffering from seemingly-intractable political, cultural and economic turmoil... and struggling to be born into a tenuous future on uncertain threads of hope and despair.

Rapid introduction of technology, educational systems, health care systems and social order have succeeded before – balancing competition and consumption in a new kind of community – and might be made to work again.

In this startling synthesis, Mr. Satterlee brings together and introduces:
- historical records,
- the social theories of the Catholic Church,
- the management theories of Peter Drucker,
- the psychosocial theories of Don Beck's Spiral Dynamics Integral, and
- the economics ideas of William Lewis and the McKinsey Global Institute on "the power of productivity."

He examines the guided development of a **virtuous web of social and economic controls**, and suggests that an unprecedented experiment in **progressive community-building** may have once created, in the deepest jungles of Uruguay, that rarest of cultural treasures – a **functional and stable utopia**... ended only by outside pressures of conquest and exploitation.

104 N Main St
PO Box 198
Dayton, IA 50530

First Wordsmith Services trade paperback edition
July, 2013

Cover Art: Blaeu, W.J. - *Paraguay, o Prov. de Rio de la Plata cum regionibus adiacentibus Tucuman et S.ta Cruz de la Sierra*, published in Amsterdam, 1645.

ISBN-13: 978-1490532653
ISBN-10: 149053265X

CreateSpace Independent Publishing Platform

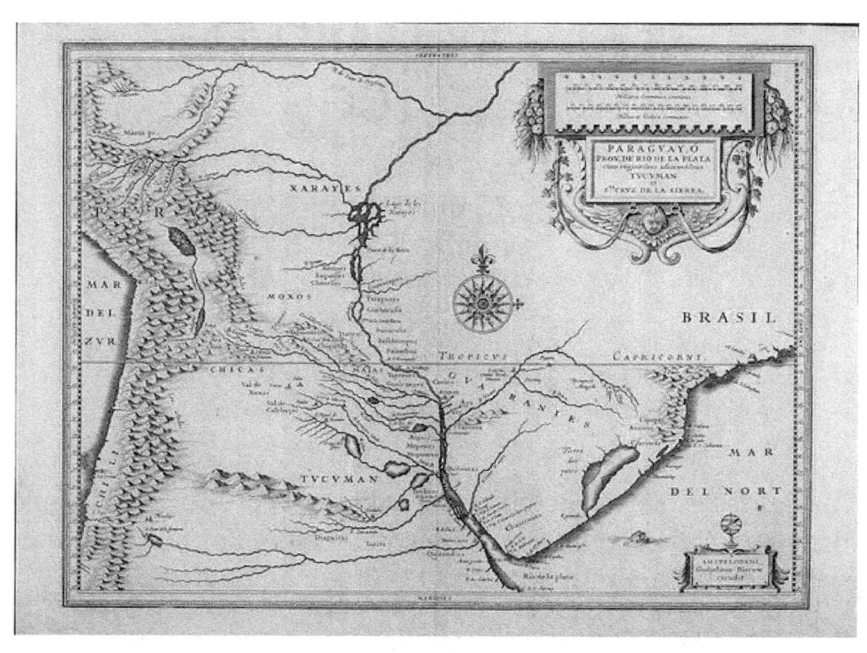

Follow at:
DavidSatterlee.blogspot.com
@DavidSatterlee
@ChumForThought
SocioDynamics.org
facebook.com/david.satterlee

Table of Contents

The Role of Productivity in Community Success:
The Jesuit-Guaraní Cultural Confluence

The European imperialistic conquests of native peoples in the "New World" tended to be brutal and destructive. This paper describes a rare instance of cultural confluence that turned out better than most... for a while. The Guaraní were the native peoples found by Spain and Portugal along the inland Paraguay River in South America. Their isolation and situation allowed for the development of a rare and revealing social experiment.

Premise

While it lasted, the success of the Jesuit-Guaraní culture in early Paraguay was the result of increased productivity. Productivity is the result of a web of factors that form a precarious balance.

Seven factors are needed in order to sustain productivity. These are: (1) a favorable environment, (2) strong and wise leadership, (3) common goals, (4) exchange of goods, (5) peace, (6) a culture of progress, and (7) improvements in technology.

Catholic Jesuit missionaries took a strong leadership role, and tailored a benevolent administration to the needs of the indigenous Guaraní. Jesuit missionaries succeeded by modeling "four central themes from [modern] Catholic social thought: (1) option for the poor; (2) human dignity; (3) the common good; and (4) solidarity" (O'Brien 397).

Until disrupted by disease, slave raids, and the removal of the Jesuits, the system prospered. When the above essential social and productivity elements of their adapted society were undermined, their society declined and collapsed.

Collisions of Cultures

Geographic isolation of otherwise similar groups produces distinctive differences. Over time, languages change beyond recognition, divergent traditions accumulate, and laws and customs are adopted to meet the needs for survival and community cohesion. The success of any group allows disposable income and time for the advancement of literacy, arts, technological experimentation, and exploration. These different levels of advancement can produce dramatic differences in world views.

Throughout human history, clans, tribes, and civilizations, each with distinctive expectations and cultures, have collided. In the grand flow of history, cultural interactions are like the confluences of streams and rivers as they gather to the seas. It cannot be unusual for neighbors, merchants, and explorers to meet and interact. In almost every case, goods, technology, genes, language, and culture have been exchanged.

The Guaraní-Colonizer Confrontation

One instance of cultural mixing occurred when Portuguese and Spanish explorers began establishing settlement outposts along the coasts and rivers of South America. European colonizers established trading posts, plantations, and new communities, often displacing indigenous groups such as the Guaraní.

Rich sources of precious metals were found in some areas. Africans were brought in and impressed into slavery to colonial masters. Natives were also made slaves or poor peons and used to exploit natural resources (Duiker 488).

Fundamentally, the colonizers were a rough and self-serving lot. They were after adventure, profits from trade, escape from misdeeds at home, or all of the above. Raw materials were exported to Europe and manufactured goods brought back in return. The natives generally considered them devils and despised the word "Christian."

Perversely enough, some among the Europeans felt strongly that they had an obligation to bring salvation to the natives by converting them to Catholicism. It was inevitable that the Guaraní natives would be influenced by Spanish and Portuguese colonization. I am not so much concerned about whether their existing culture should or should not have been influenced; that was inevitable. Rather, I want to explore the characteristics of the modified culture that allowed it to grow and prosper for over a century.

Europeans from Spain first settled well upriver on the bank of the Paraguay River when Gonzalo de Mendoza founded Asuncion in 1537. Within two years the Guaraní tried and failed to destroy the new settlement. Asuncion was used as a base for inland expeditions in 1542 and 1548 to find rumored silver mines. These mines turned out to have already been discovered by the Spanish as they explored inland from the Pacific. Offspring of Spanish colonizers and native women became a neo-American "Paraguayan" population who identified with European culture but spoke Guaraní (Riberio 397).

The Guaraní-Jesuit Confluence

Jesuits—Catholic monks of the Order of Jesus—committed themselves to further the economic, political, and spiritual interests of the Church. Jesuits established a successful series of missions along the more inaccessible upper reaches of South American river systems. These missions often blossomed into "mission states," which operated independently from secular governors (Duiker 488, 489).

Initial missionary work among the Guaraní was conducted by Franciscans. Eighteen mission communities were developed among the Guaraní by Luis de Bolanos, a Franciscan, between the 1560s and 1580s. He developed settlements, which attracted numerous individuals and tribes to live in their relative comfort and safety. An on-site missionary acted as a patriarchal local governor. The communities were called "Reductions" from the Portuguese word reducer, meaning "to gather together."

One of the first things the Jesuits undertook was to free indigenous (but not African) slaves. Of course, this move was unpopular among the colonists, who felt that use of the natives was their right and essential to their success.

Next, beginning in 1609, Jesuits took over responsibility for missions to the Guaraní. They learned the Guaraní language and came with a sense of respect. Although the Jesuits assumed a paternal role, they chose to recruit, lead, and collaborate, rather than dominate.

These Jesuit missionaries succeeded in cultivating peaceful, altruistic, and benevolent relationships with the native peoples they found. The Jesuits' areas of influence were centered on cultivating village communes where survival was easier, agriculture assured a regular food supply, and communal work provided income and access to manufactured goods.

The result was profitable for these native communities. The Jesuits "...brought Indians together into villages where the natives could be converted, taught trades, and encouraged to grow crops. ... The Catholic church built hospitals, orphanages, and schools that instructed Indian students..." (Duiker 489).

The Jesuits created a prosperous true communist society, which lasted for about 150 years. Although not true egalitarianism, the established goal was an acceptable sense of fairness among the population. The political "state" was invested in the curate, who managed secular issues, and his sub-curate who managed spiritual matters. Both kept a low profile and worked through male intermediaries.

Although work was required from the natives who chose to live in the community, work was light and festivals were abundant. All production benefited the community, with surplus being sold to obtain outside goods. Every "citizen" was provided for generously (Duiker 490).

Thomas O'Brien wrote that "...the most compelling characteristic of the Guaraní/Jesuit communities was their capacity to manage the inevitable collision of two disparate peoples in such a way that often the best of both societies arose in what eventually became a hybrid civilization... [achieved] ...through hard and patient work by both the Guaraní and the Jesuits" (O'Brien 396).

The History of Guaraní Culture in Confluence

The Guaraní Before Contact

When they initially met The first European explorers, the Guaraní lived in independent groups of about 20 families; sometimes polygamously. They hunted, kept animals and, using wooden tools, raised a few simple crops. They were semi-nomadic; conflicts between groups were not uncommon. They cannibalized prisoners of war (O'Brien 398).

European Colonization in South America

Initially, the Portuguese concentrated on the spice trade in the Indies by sailing around the horn of Africa. Christopher Columbus, however, sailing under the flag of Spain, tried to reach the same goal by repeatedly sailing west starting in 1492. In 1494, the Spanish and Portuguese, in the Treaty of Tordesillas, had already divided the world into areas of influence. Spain first explored the Rio de la Plata (leading up into the Guaraní area and modern Paraguay) in 1511 (Juan de Solis), and returned in 1526 (Sebastian Cabot). In other areas, Hernán Cortés overthrew the Aztec empire in central

Mexico by 1522 and Francisco Pizarro conquered the Incan empire by 1536 (Duiker 370).

The Spanish introduced cattle and horses, which rapidly reproduced into large herds. Wild cattle were, at first, public property and useful for meat, tallow, and skins. Eventually, control of these cattle became a divisive issue that contributed to regional conflicts (Rebeiro 398).

Expansion of Settlements among the Guaraní

During the 1560-80s, Franciscan priests established eighteen communities among the Guaraní. The Jesuit Order (The Society of Jesus) was not even formed until 1540. However, the Jesuits became effective "points of the sword" where the church had special needs and were soon sent to North and South American frontiers. (See "The Jesuit Order," below.) The first Jesuits arrived in 1585 and established themselves for about 15 years before opening new missions.

Jesuit Intervention with the Guaraní

After gradually building their influence in the area, the Jesuits spent another forty years actively building a network of Jesuit-run Guaraní Reductions (mission-towns). They successfully operated these Reductions, unobstructed for ninety years, before serious disease and outside political and military intervention began to interfere with their design. It took another one hundred years for the society that they built to collapse. By the end, the Guaraní were thoroughly decimated, assimilated and dispersed.

In 1606 the Jesuits are credited with forming the Province of Paraguay. Two years later, they succeeded in freeing the

Indian slaves in Paraguay. They followed this in 1609 by forming their first new Reduction (mission). This was successful and for the next few decades, the Jesuits began to found missions on the Paranapanema River above the Guaira Falls. Natives were invited to join the Reductions on the condition that they submit to its rules.

These mission towns were built around a central square with the church as the centerpiece. Other community buildings such as schools, storehouses, and guesthouses were also built near the center. Spreading out, each family had use of lodgings in long adobe buildings. The land was divided into assigned portions. Harvests not only supported those doing the growing, but were stored in common storehouses and shared by all members of the community. The surplus was used to trade for tools, salt, and other necessities. Guaraní natives raised livestock, farmed, sold maté tea, made cloth and musical instruments. To maintain order, the Jesuits were known to use corporal punishment, but the threat of expulsion was usually effective.

The Slave Wars

During the 1620-30s, almost a dozen missions above the fall line were eradicated by Portuguese "Paulista" slave raiders from Sao Paulo. They took slaves, looted the missions and took trade goods, cattle, and Church valuables. Many Jesuits and Guaraní were forced to relocate downriver. Slave raids ended in 1641 when Guaraní and Jesuits successfully defeated slave raiders at Mbobore on the Acaray River.

Guaraní Mission Prosperity

During the next ninety years, the missions mostly enjoyed an enviable abundance and peace. At their peak in 1732, there were about 30 missions with a total population of over 140,000. These were guarded by army of over 7,000. This is a remarkable achievement and is credited to good will and collaboration between the Jesuits, the Guaraní peoples, and their leaders. Together, they created communities that have been repeatedly compared to the realization of ageless utopian visions.

The Beginning of the End

Colonial hostilities broke out periodically. Guaraní missions were used as soldier's encampments and Guaraní men were recruited for the fighting. The Europeans were "notorious for lack of hygiene; soldiers carried disease with them and died in large numbers in encampments" (Jackson 402). This led to decades of smallpox epidemics, which severely weakened the Guaraní communities. In 1734 a smallpox epidemic killed 30,000.

During 1743, the Jesuits in two missions undertook to build new, large, and very sturdy churches, greater than would have been needed to serve the needs of their mission. These may have been intended to help resist any future Portuguese attacks (Jackson 404). They did not know it, but within another 42 years, the Spanish would force all Jesuits to leave the area. The Jesuit control, and the virtuous web of productivity within their missions, would be broken.

In 1750, the Treaty of Madrid was signed to resolve regional political squabbling. It redrew the border between Spanish and Portuguese territories; thousands of people were displaced. Guaraní were specifically required to relocate.

Refugees from Portuguese settlements to the east fled upriver and destabilized those missions. The Guaraní resisted Spanish and Portuguese troops trying to enforce the Treaty of Madrid. They fared badly and, in seven missions, the population dispersed and declined by half (Jackson 404).

The End of Paradise

In 1763, the Spanish used the missions while invading Portuguese settlements. Shortly thereafter, another smallpox epidemic killed 12,000 people.

The Spanish King Carlos III evicted Jesuits from all of Spain's territories, including Paraguay, in 1767. Monks of the Franciscan order took over direction of the missions. Without the tight control exercised by the Jesuits, inefficiency and corruption eroded the attraction of the missions and many Guaraní left. The missions continued to decline despite the relative peace that lasted for another forty years.

By the end of the eighteenth century many mission Indians had dispersed or been enslaved. Some dissolved into the world of the gauchos or else became refugees in the wilderness, where they struggled to reconstitute their tribal life. Their lands and cattle passed into the hands of new owners (Ribeiro 398).

Peace was broken again in1801 when the Portuguese army invaded and occupied many missions. By that time, the mission population had declined to only 45,000 Guaraní. Nonetheless the Guaraní, led by Andresito Guacurari counter-attacked and won some early battles. By 1814, however, only 8,000 were left in the missions. By 1821, mission lands had been devastated and the Guaraní conceded defeat.

As if this was not enough, a six-year war from 1864 to 1870 between Paraguay and its neighbors, Brazil, Uruguay, and Argentina, caught what was left of the Guaraní in the middle. The few left in the missions were killed or dispersed.

A Brief History of the Jesuit Order

The Society of Jesus was founded in 1540 by Ignatius of Loyola and approved by Pope Paul III. Collectively called "Jesuits," the new order was organized in a hierarchical military model and provided rigorous training to their recruits. The Jesuits followed a theocratic system that was thoroughly organized and strictly obedient to the Jesuit fathers. Their work was "the propagation and strengthening of the Catholic faith everywhere." They often served as special-needs troubleshooters. The Jesuits were initially highly-regarded and "immediately in great request to instruct the faithful, and to reform the clergy, monasteries, and convents" (Pollen, par. 1). They succeeded in "recruiting some of the best and brightest young men of Europe as missionaries" (Bach 211).

The success of the Jesuits in Paraguay may have contributed to their downfall. The missions directly opposed exploitation by colonies of Spain and Portugal. Jesuits were accused of creating a "Christian republic" with the intention of declaring independence (Ribeiro 398). Other monastic orders of the church became jealous of the success and power of the Jesuits as well (Jaenike 275).

The Jesuits were not just successful in South America. They had amassed a great deal of political and economic influence wherever they worked, including Europe. Naturally, they made enemies. The King of Spain expelled the Jesuits from all Spanish territories, including Paraguay, in 1768. Pope Benedict XIV, shortly before his death in 1759, was pressured to order an investigation of the Jesuits. This led to their suppression in Portugal. Their order was dissolved by Pope Clement XIV in 1773. Following restabilization of European monarchs, the Jesuit order was reconstituted in 1814 by Pope Pius VII. (Pollen, History)

Vital Social Virtues

The Jesuit-Guaraní system had more going for it than the above-mentioned seven productivity factors. Thomas O'Brien describes "four central themes from [modern] Catholic social thought: (1) option for the poor; (2) human dignity; (3) the common good; and (4) solidarity" (O'Brien 397). Although these themes are the product of more modern theological thought, they may reflect a "genuine timeless quality ... harvested from the religious ideals associated with the ideal Reign of God found in the Christian Scriptures" (O'Brien 400). The Jesuit missions seem to have already embraced these philosophies.

Option for the Poor

"Option for the poor" reflects the sense that God loves all people equally and that God, in caring for the poor, desires to see them raised up to full inclusion with their brothers. Worldly wealth and power were not to be allowed to exclude the weak and needy. The Jesuits directly opposed European colonizers by freeing native slaves, establishing safe refuge for natives in the Reductions, and increasing the economic security available to the Guaraní peoples. The Jesuits believed that these communities became the "vessels, signs and sacraments" of Christ's saving reign and grace (O'Brien 402).

Common Good

"Common good" directs that governing authority be responsible for assuring that all aspects of community life serve the best interests of the entire group. This principle assured that everyone embraced by the community had, not just subsistence needs, but a "fair share" compared to their neighbors. Many individuals were thereby freed to take up trades, manufacturing goods that were redistributed within the community or traded for other manufactured items. Arts and community infrastructure projects were managed in the same way. While individuals certainly sometimes hoarded or engaged in black-market trading, the possibility of corporal punishment or expulsion seemed to keep self-seeking adequately under control. Unlike most civilizations, a self-enriching aristocracy did not arise during Jesuit control. Evidently, the Guaraní chose to embrace the common goal of common good (O'Brian 403).

Solidarity

The Jesuits enforced Guaraní as the common language and created a written form of the language as well. They allowed native customs to have a marked impact on evolving culture, arts, and even religious traditions. Typically, Europeans landed, colonized, conquered, subordinated, and minimized. Natives were sometimes allowed to assimilate, but it was largely a one-way process. With the Guaraní, the priests introduced elements of European culture and allowed a synthesis to develop, rather than imposing their foreign culture unilaterally. Although the Jesuits accommodated the Guaraní in many ways, priests of their order took vows of obedience and were subject to a considerable hierarchy of authorities, which were very abstract to most Guaraní. However, a strong sense of mutual respect was generally maintained (O'Brian 404-405).

Human Dignity

Unlike most Europeans, the Jesuits did not consider Guaraní natives to be savage animals, but fully human children of God. They did not stand for the Guaraní to be exploited for forced labor. [One wonders, then, how the African slaves did not receive the same defense.] Further, the Jesuits recognized the crudity of their colonial compatriots and saw some elements of the Guaraní way of life as superior. The Guaraní were accorded a degree of dignity and respect that was remarkable for their times. The Europeans were clever and had shameless ambition. The natives were more innocent and, with their needs met, content to leave their neighbors in peace.

Vital Productivity Virtues

Anthropologist Marvin Harris developed a theory of "Cultural Materialism," which says that our species is evolving as

...societies with higher productivity inevitably replace societies with lower productivity... Societies with higher productivity have overcome to a greater degree whatever cultural, religious, ethnic, climatic, and political barriers have constrained productivity. These higher productivity societies have been successful in competition with lower productivity societies. They have been successful either through conquest or through simply surviving the hardships of nature (Lewis xii).

Seven factors are needed in a community in order to sustain productivity. These are: (1) a favorable environment, (2) strong and wise leadership, (3) common goals, (4) exchange of goods, (5) peace, (6) a culture of progress, and (7) improvements in technology. These factors are examined next, with examples from the operation of Guaraní Reductions.

Favorable Environment

A favorable environment directly supports productivity. It is easier to do a thing if more of it can be done with fewer resources. If the soil and climate are favorable, your crops will grow more abundantly. For instance, Jared Diamond in *Guns, Germs, and Steel: The Fates of Human Societies* asserts that the combination of abundant domesticatable wild grains during times of declining wildlife encouraged bands of hunter-gathers to transition to agriculture, and stimulated the rise of civilizations in China and Europe (Diamond 110, 1999). Because imported cattle became abundant and the climate was temperate, both wildlife and crops were easier to acquire.

Peace

Earlier wars of conquest and plunder usually paid survival dividends for the winner. World War II is generally credited for lifting the United States out of depression: war can be terribly focusing and motivating. Nonetheless, wars of defense or aggression wastefully consume resources better directed to more productive pursuits.

Productivity reduces one's survival issues, which reduces the incentive to prey on neighbors. Neighbors, who are not preying on you, allow you to commit your energies to increasing production of goods. The Jesuit missions produced more peaceful relationships among Guaraní groups. The Jesuits prohibited cannibalism, and improved living standards and security so that there was no longer any need to attack neighbors for survival.

Success breeds envy. The secular European colonies coveted the goods, economic success, and political independence of the Reductions. Colonists relied on forced labor for their plantations; Reductions took thousands of potential indigenous laborers off the market.

Exchange of Goods

Trade with your neighbors allows you to import and become familiar with their technologies. If you can easily replicate it, you can use this new technology to improve quantity, quality, or efficiency. Trading can increase productivity by helping you to obtain materials that you could not otherwise make efficiently for yourself. Trade with neighbors is a strong motivation to make peace, not war. The Jesuits also maintained tight control over all aspects of trade with those outside of their Reduction.

Strong, Wise Leadership

A good leader has courage, insight, wisdom, and strength. He will organize and motivate his community around common goals such as a culture of progress, compassion for the misfortune of others, investment in education, arts, technology, infrastructure, and harmonious trade.

The Guaraní were used to governing themselves with a light hand. The authority of their chiefs and shamans were as honored servants of the tribes and by consent of the group. This is reminiscent of Luke 9:48: "And [Jesus] said unto them, Whosoever shall receive this child in my name receiveth me: and whosoever shall receive me receiveth him that sent me: for he that is least among you all, the same shall be great" (KJV). Although some priests were condescending and distrustful, the Jesuits seem to have approached their "stewardship" of the Guaraní with a similar humility.

The Jesuits recognized the importance of winning the trust, cooperation, and collaboration of the tribal chieftains. They embraced an old Spanish proverb: "The flock will be like its shepherd." They recognized the value of recruiting the existing shepherds and serving as wise shepherds themselves (Bach).

The Jesuit priests exercised the ultimate managerial authority within a Reduction. They delegated responsibilities as they saw fit. The benevolent autarchy of the Jesuits included coercion as necessary. A priest might direct a Guaraní leader to administer caning to another Guaraní. The heaviest threat was to be put out of the community. Capital punishment was not used.

Common Goals

Common goals will encourage pursuit of all elements of the virtuous, productive web. Common goals can include appreciation for literacy, technology, arts, peace, and ethical work for the common good.

Guaraní Reductions emphasized communal work and collaboration. Crops and livestock were cared for cooperatively. In time, a wide range of programs including textiles, raising maté, and even manufacture of musical instruments, became organized community projects. O'Brien points out that the Reduction model did not succeed with some other peoples in both North and South America. He concludes that: "...the decisive factor at work in the success of the Guaraní Reductions was the cooperation of the Guaraní themselves" (O'Brien 399).

Literacy

Literacy contributes to a culture of progress and facilitates technical development, trade, and the training of craftsmen. Literary is especially vital for community leaders, record keepers, and teachers. Literate citizens enjoy a richer life and are better prepared to contribute to community advancement.

Each mission included schools for boys and girls. Depending on their abilities, they were taught trades (carpentry, pottery, weaving, or decorative arts) or to read. Some, selected for future responsibilities, also learned Spanish or Latin.

Advances in Technology

New technologies can improve the manufacture, quality, storage, and transportation of goods. Improved technology can produce stronger weapons, used defensively to sustain peace.

Jared Diamond also points out that new technologies for collecting, processing, and storing agricultural harvests were essential for exploiting and domesticating wild grains. He describes this as an "autocatalytic process—one that catalyzes itself in a positive feedback cycle, going faster and faster once it has started." Increased technology led to increased technology, with the result of allowing increased population density (Diamond, "Guns" 111).

Productivity Gives Back

Productivity frees up time and resources to engage in artistic pursuits. Arts are often in demand as trade goods. Time freed from pursuing survival needs can also be devoted to developing new technology.

Rather than accumulating riches for a few, the missions reinvested the wealth that was generated. The communities prospered; public works for sanitation, housing, and worship were constructed. Often the streets were bricked. The system rewarded individual devotion and production on merit. Talents were encouraged among children and adults. Although there was no private ownership, the community prospered. The mission system even acquired its own sea-going ships for trade.

The Need for Community

In the introduction to the book *The Community of the Future*, Peter Drucker describes a "problem" with our modern cities. Rural communities, by their limited size and increased familiarity, are intrusive, and coercive. People know you, know the history of your family, and have strong expectations for your behavior. Many people want the city's freedom, independence, autonomy, and possibility for upward mobility. But, he points out: "...beneath that thin layer of professionals, artists, scholars, the wealthy and the highly skilled artisans in their craft guilds, there was moral and social anomie, prostitution, banditry, and lawlessness" (Drucker 2). Also: "If no communities are available for constructive ends, there will be destructive, murderous communities... gangs that today threaten the very social fabric of the large...cities" (Drucker 3). Drucker explains that "community" arises from family, religion, social class, or caste. He asserts that the social programs of national governments have failed to supply the needs of urban societies but that effective communities can, and must, be found or founded (Drucker 5).

Disaster vs. Development

In his book, *Collapse, How Societies Choose to Fail or Succeed*, Jared Diamond surveys a wide range of civilizations and their ultimate collapse. He identified several factors common to inadequate group decision making.

First, a group may fail to anticipate a problem before the problem actually arrives. Second, when the problem does arrive, the group may fail to perceive it. Then, after they perceive it, they may fail even to try to solve it. Finally, they may try to solve it but may not succeed (Diamond, "Collapse" 421).

Human development psychologist Clare Graves identified another factor common to human communities. He observed that they naturally develop through a predictable hierarchy of world views, They subsequently need to adjust as they—and their citizens, and their neighbors—lurch gradually from one set of societal expectations to the next. This process of development destabilizes from inside and out; every successful human community will have to adjust over time to accommodate.

In interpreting the research of Clare Graves, Don Beck and Christopher Cowan point out that "different times produce different minds." They see individuals, organizations and societies maturing from survival needs to tribal kinship-mysticism, power-independence, purpose-order-obedience, achieve-create-succeed-conquer, science-winning-good life, sensitivity-equality, dynamic integration-flow, and ecological holism. (Beck 33, 41-47). Individuals who have achieved higher personal levels are better-equipped to govern communities that operate on lower levels. Individuals operating from earlier levels just cannot understand what the ideals of higher levels are about. The good news is that human social systems have continued to trend toward greater maturity and development over the centuries. As an indication of the success of this concept, Beck and Cowan were instrumental consultants in South Africa's successful move away from apartheid.

Conclusion

Every ecosystem exists in a tension between individual self-determinism and the need for webs of relationships. Communities form ecologies to support the needs of both individuals and the overall community. Successful communities enhance the well-being of their voluntary members.

Occasionally, circumstance will bring together serendipitous conditions and people. The Jesuits and the Guaraní were ready for each other and had values to complement each other. The priests offered a system of security and abundance within a harmonious community. Before, the Guaraní were just only surviving in smaller groups and ready to expand their options.

The Guaraní-Jesuit collaboration increased productivity in a way that enriched their communities, rather than individuals. This allowed for a virtuous web of social and economic controls to build upon itself. This rare success continued for as long as they were able to keep themselves isolated from intimate contact with the disruptive aggression and greed of outsiders. They almost managed to save themselves.

Darcy Ribeiro finds a parallel in more modern times with Japan's post-feudal period:

A long time afterwards, in better conditions, Japan revived the Paraquayan type of despotic, autonomist state orientation, demonstrating its viability as one of the few roads to autonomous industrialization and national emancipation within the industrial-imperialistic system of domination (Ribeiro 404).

Peter Drucker, who helped the Japanese re-industrialize after World War II, confesses:

More than fifty years ago, in my 1943 book, *The Future of Industrial Man*, I proposed what I then called the 'self-governing plant community,' the community within the new social organization, the large business enterprise. It has worked, but only in one country, Japan. It is clear that even there, this is not the answer, not the solution (Drucker 5).

The Guaraní-Jesuit communities were just as Drucker proposes for successful, productive urban communities: free and voluntary, although intrusive and coercive. These communities give evidence that, what we cannot achieve as individuals, we have the potential to more-productively achieve through voluntary cooperation toward the common good.

Works Cited

Bach, Caleb. "Journal from a Jesuit Frontier." Americas 49.6 (Nov 1007): MAS Ultra-School Edition. EBSCO 21 Jan. 2009

Beck, Don and Christopher Cowan. Spiral Dynamics: Mastering values, leadership, and change. Blackwell Publishers, Cambridge and Oxford, 1996

Diamond, Jared M, Jonathan Cape. Guns, Germs, and Steel: the fates of human societies. W. Norton & Company, 1999

Diamond, Jared M. Collapse: How societies choose to fail or succeed, Penguin Books, 2006

Duiker, William J., Jackson J. Spielvogel; World History Volume Two: Since 1500,3rd ed. Belmont: Wadsworth/Thomson Learning, 2001

Hesselbein, Goldsmith and Beckhard, Editors. The Community of the Future,. The Drucker Foundation, Jossey-Bass, San Francisco, 1997

Jackson, Robert H. "The Population and Vital Rates of the Jesuit Missions of Paraguay", 1700-1767. Journal of Interdisciplinary History, xxxviii:3. Winter, 2008

Jaenike, William F. Black Robes in Paraguay: The Success of the Guaraní Missions Hastened the Abolition of the Jesuits. Kirk House Publishers, Minneapolis: 2008

Lewis, William W. The Power of Productivity: Wealth, Poverty, and the Threat to Global Stability, The University of Chicago Press, 2004

Pollen, John Hungerford. "The Society of Jesus." <u>The Catholic Encyclopedia</u>. Vol. 14. New York: Robert Appleton Company, 1912. 20 Feb. 2009

Pollen, John Hungerford."History of the Jesuits Before the 1773 Suppression."<u>The Catholic Encyclopedia.</u>. 14.York: Robert Appleton Company,.Feb. 2009

Rubeurim, Darcy. <u>The Americas and Civilization</u>, trans. Linton Lomas Barrett and Marie McDavid Barrett. New York: E. P. Dutton, 1972

More books from David Satterlee:

Chum for Thought: Throwing Ideas into Dangerous Waters

Filled with essays drawn from his columns in the *Dayton Review* and other writings (including this work). Explores the cultural differences and conjunctions between conservative and liberal values.

"Somehow both an agnostic and true believer, he radiates optimism — still seeking illumination in dark places. His favorite themes are community, virtues, values, and growth. He will tease you into his world and then send you off to explore your own."

Life Will Get You in the End: Short Stories by David Satterlee

"[His writing is] humorous, bold, and adventurous all at once ... channeled through a facility for language and the music of words."

Each story is short and sweet – or sometimes bittersweet – or just thought-provoking. Put your best teeth in and prepare to enjoy each snack-sized portion. There's usually a little surprise in the last bite. I'll bet that you will sometimes read a story again right away. I guarantee that you will come back to some of your favorites over and over... and recommend them to your friends.

Honoring My Father: Coming to Terms

In this heartfelt account, David Satterlee tells personal stories of a remarkable father, his own failure in family and faith... and the rediscovery of love worth living for.

YOU are a vital part of marketing for a new generation of self-published authors. *Thank you for buying and reading this book!*

And, if you would be so kind, **please let others know** why you recommend it. This is how much of publishing works now. Thank you, thank you, thank you.

Follow at:
DavidSatterlee.blogspot.com
@DavidSatterlee
@ChumForThought
SocioDynamics.org
facebook.com/david.satterlee